How To
RELEASE
YOUR
FAITH?

Rev J Martin

DEDICATION

I dedicate this book to my family, for their constant love and support.

CONTENTS

ACKNOWLEDGMENTS

This book would not have been possible without the support and encouragement of my family, and the inspiration from my Heavenly Father.

A special thanks to: my editor; Pixal Design Studios for the design work, and Amazon for providing the digital tools by which I can get my message out into the world.

Finally, I would like to thank YOU, for buying my book, may it enlighten your life and bring you peace.

Introduction

Something most of us share is we don't like change, the reason being that life is easier when things remain the same. A similar routine is comforting as it limits the stress and worries of life. So that can seem like a good thing, but it's not.

In the last twelve months many changes have been forced on us; I can only speak for myself, but I have found it challenging. I've noticed that my mood can quickly change. Usually a relaxed and calm person, I now get irritated and annoyed quickly.

When I reflected on the reason why, I became aware that most of my conversations were the same— talking about the virus, how it affected everyone, and listening to people worried and afraid for the future. No matter how strong your faith, enough fear can break down your defenses.

It's easy for me to advise you to avoid the news and avoid social media, but, as humans, we yearn for answers; we want to be aware of the potential dangers and keep our family and friends safe. Protecting the people close to us is our primal nature.

So, what can we do? We need to learn to renew our minds so that our faith can be released.

Many verses in scripture refer to the renewal of our minds, but what exactly does that mean? The renewal of your mind means the shedding of old, limiting, fearful thoughts and replacing them with thoughts of faith, hope and gratitude.

When you awake each morning, you get to choose how you approach the day. You can rush out of bed and decide whether to check your phone or take a walk outside. You get to determine if you will sit in silence eating breakfast or watch the news. You get to choose to ring your friend who is always negative or the friend who lifts your spirits and makes you feel better.

Each day you have the choice to renew your mind with new thinking. However, the problem most people have is they keep making the same decisions day after day. They keep the same routine and then wonder why nothing ever changes. Often, we limit ourselves without even knowing it. We go around thinking that the obstacle is too big, that we will never get well, that the virus will get the best of us. We replay the same thoughts continuously in our minds and then we wonder why we are stressed and don't have any strength; our thoughts limit us. We can get easily lost in what we constantly think about.

The Bible says as a man thinks in his heart, so he is. So, you can't expect to think thoughts of fear and live a life of faith. You can't expect to think weak thoughts and have strength. And you cannot expect to think thoughts of defeat and experience victory.

To renew your mind, you must take in new information. Success and happiness depend on your thinking. Most people's attitude is, "Well, the pandemic has me afraid, I'm worried about my health; I'm stressed over my children. I'm anxious about my future."

Of course, these are genuine concerns, but if these are your daily thoughts, that line of thinking will draw in more negativity, which will make you weaker, draining your strength, energy, and passion.

You will be amazed at what can happen when you start to freshen up your mind with new thinking. You will feel strength rising up from within that will give you courage, determination, and the confidence to manifest God's promises in your life.

Romans 12:2

Do not conform to the pattern of this world but be transformed by the renewing of your mind. Then you will be able to test and approve what God's will is—his good, pleasing and perfect will.

Rearview Mirror

The Apostle Paul went through a lot of adversity; he was falsely accused, put in prison, beaten with rods, and shipwrecked, often going days without food.

And yet in Philippians 3.13 (TLB) he said, "I'm still not all I should be, but I am bringing all my energies to bear this one thing, forgetting the past and looking forward to what lies ahead."

He could have said, "I will focus all my energy on being a better leader, speaker, and writer," but instead, he said, in effect, "What is more important than all that is letting go of what lies behind and pressing forward."

After all he had been through, he had the right to be discouraged, with the attitude, "Look what happened to me, it's not fair." But he had learnt that you need to let go of the past if you want to move forward.

What if we would do like Paul and start focusing our energy on dropping the offence, dropping the guilt, dropping the self-pity, dropping that hurt and moving forward?

How do you drop the past? Renew your mind with new thinking.

Apostle Paul didn't focus on the people who wrongly accused him or put him in prison; he focused on God. He didn't replay old hurts in his mind day after day, talking about his misfortune to everyone he met. He put his attention on how he could become a better Christian.

The reason why some people never heal is they are always opening old wounds. Every week they rehash with their friends, "Can you believe what so and so did to me?" They might have been hurt ten years ago, but they are still dragging it up as though it happened yesterday. Don't rehearse negative things that happened to you. Put them away once and for all. Decide today not to spend any more time thinking or talking about them.

The betrayal, the disappointment, the injustice is in the past. If you keep picking at it, the wound will never heal. People will listen once or twice, but if you are always talking about what happened in the past, people will not want to be around you. Years ago, I worked with someone who always complained; everything seemed to go wrong for him. Rarely did he ever have anything good to say. Even though he had worked for the company for many years, he couldn't understand why he never got promoted. A negative attitude can stop you from fulfilling your destiny.

When you are mad at somebody, offended at your neighbour, carrying around unforgiveness and bitterness, you may not realise it but that negative attitude pushes people and opportunities away.

When the annoyance, the mistake, the hurt plays on the movie screen of your mind, do yourself a favour, change the channel. Say, "I'm not going backwards, living in regret; I'm not rehearsing the painful events of my life. From today I choose to move forward."

A good way of renewing your mind is to pay attention to what you are dwelling on all day. Listen to what you are saying. How much time and energy are you giving to the negative feelings of your past—guilt, offence, blame, discouragement?

We have a limited amount of emotional energy each day, so when you spend that energy on negative things like calling a friend and talking about what somebody did to you three years ago, or rehearsing your failures, or focusing on negative events, you are using energy that you should be using to move forward. You must get out of what was and step into what is.

Don't say another word about that breakup, that disappointment, that setback you went through. Don't tell another person about the mistake you made; that is over and done with. Don't relive those losses one more time in your mind. You determine what you think about.

The difference between positive people and people who are negative is simple. People who are negative hold on to the past, while positive people have learnt to let go of the past and move forward into the good things that God has in store.

Bad Quality Recording

Once, I met a young lady who was very down on herself; she told me that she felt unattractive. She was dealing with an eating disorder, which no one else knew about.

She was very well dressed and beautiful in appearance, but she had let a negative recording play, and it became stuck in her head. Over and over, she was hearing, *You're not attractive, you're overweight. Nobody cares about you.*

All lies, but our minds are very powerful; a wrong recording can destroy your life. She had all the natural beauty in the world. Her problem was that the negative recording had made her feel unattractive on the inside.

It turned out she had been bullied at school. Jealous girls had teased her so much that she believed their lies. I advised her that she needed to renew her mind with new thinking. She needed to change the recording she was playing day after day.

Instead of replaying what the bullies said years ago, she needed to replay what her family and friends said about her—that she was beautiful, confident, intelligent, and valuable.

Most people think, *If only I can look good on the outside, I will feel good on the inside,* but very often, it's the opposite. If you can feel good on the inside and play the correct recording, you will look good on the outside. You will be happy, contented and have peace of mind.

We all spend time each morning getting dressed ready for our day. We put effort into looking good on the outside. And that's good. But a pretty face can't hide low confidence. Wearing the latest fashion can't hide feeling depressed.

I wonder what would happen if we spent time each morning getting our spirit ready for the day. If we said to ourselves before we left the house, "I am strong, I am talented; I am disciplined, focused, and beautiful."

These positive affirmations will get your inner recording started in the right direction, and the more you replay them the more the recording will become a part of you. Just as negativity will get you down, positivity will lift you up. And the more you dwell on the right thoughts the less room there is for the wrong thoughts.

One way the enemy works against us is he tries to plant lies in our minds to infect our thinking. *You're not good enough; you're not attractive. You will never meet the right person.*

We can try to change things on the outside, but until we get to the root of the problem, until we change the negative thoughts, they will continue to limit us.

Months later, I met the same young lady, now walking with such confidence. When we got chatting, she started crying saying that she could never repay me. She was eating normally and now returning to college to further her education.

Simply changing a negative recording can have such an impact on your life. So instead of replaying past hurts, past regrets, and past mistakes, I encourage you to change the recording to, "I am talented; I am valuable; I have the grace of God."

Outside My Comfort Zone

A few months before my father died, he asked me to renovate part of his house. Everyone thought he was crazy as he was in the latter stages of COPD (chronic obstructive pulmonary disease), but I knew it was a job he had meant to do but kept putting off.

The job would involve dealing with contractors, electricians, plumbers, and decorators. I didn't think I was capable, but my father believed I could do it, and I didn't want to let him down. Instantly my mind filled with negative, fearful, intimidating thoughts. Each thought told me I couldn't do it; I wasn't qualified; I couldn't organise and overlook the work. I had to do what I'm recommending you do. When the negative thoughts would come to my mind, I didn't focus on them believing they were true. I faded them out and filled my mind with faith. Purposely I changed the recording, thinking, *I can do all things through Christ; I have been raised up to do great things, I am strong in the Lord. I am equipped, empowered, and anointed.*

In scripture it says, be careful what you think; it gives us a warning that our thoughts are setting the limits for our life.

Weeks before my dad died, he got to see the completed job; he was thrilled and full of praise. But if I had believed the negative thoughts, I wouldn't have the memories that I hold so dear.

When faced with a challenge, you will find that negative thoughts will pour into your mind—telling you that there is no way out, that there is no point even trying. Better to stay where you are.

In moments of fear, you must renew your mind with new thinking—*I can, I will, and I must.* Release your faith and you will see the difference it makes.

Take Off Your Coat

In the scripture, it says, put on a garment of praise in a spirit of despair. Isaiah 61:3. A garment is like a coat; before you can put on a coat of faith, you must take off a coat of despair.

Sometimes we wonder why we aren't happy, why we are not passionate about life; we are wearing the wrong coat. *The world isn't fair; I never get any good breaks; I will never fulfil my destiny.* That type of thinking doesn't look good on you. The self-pity coat is out of style. The coat of bitterness over the betrayal doesn't fit you anymore. Wearing the wrong coat is restricting your spiritual growth. Now do your part and take off the coat of despair and put on the coat of praise.

"Lord, thank you that your plans for me are good. I trust in you to show me the way, guide me to make the right choices each day, so I focus on faith and not on worry and doubt."

In Ephesians 4, Apostle Paul said, "be constantly renewed in the spirit of your mind [having a fresh mental and spiritual attitude AMPC version]." Every day, he said, you need to put on a fresh new attitude because yesterday's mood will get old. If you don't start fresh and anew, you bring all the negativity from yesterday into a new day.

Apostle Paul knew the damaging effects negative thoughts could have on us, keeping us locked in the past, keeping us restricted, unable to move forward.

When you wake each morning, you need to put on a coat of praise. "Thank you, Lord, for another day. Thank you for all that I have. Everything may not be perfect, but I'm grateful to be alive. I'm thankful for my family; I'm thankful for my home; I'm grateful for all the opportunities in my life." A spirit of gratitude is the best way to start the day.

In Wrong Thinking

We've all had bad things happen to us; people mistreated us, a friend let us down, we missed an opportunity to move ahead. It's easy to go through life blaming ourselves for mistakes we've made, feeling offended and in self-pity. But when we are always looking back, reliving past hurts and disappointments, we end up carrying around a lot of negative baggage that can weigh us down. One of the best things we can do is forget about it and move on.

Whether something happened 30 years ago or 30 minutes ago, don't carry that negative baggage into a new day. It's impossible to live a happy, successful life if you are constantly replaying what didn't work out, thinking about who hurt you or about the mistakes you made. It is called the past because it's behind you, its history; now do your best to keep moving forward.

"Well, you have no idea what happened; they broke my heart; that's why I'm bitter."

Letting similar negative recordings replay over and over will keep you discouraged, resulting in you having no passion. They hurt you once; don't allow them to continue to hurt you.

There are great things in your future, but first you must forget the past. Quit thinking about it, reliving it, and move forward; there is a new beginning in front of you. We have all made mistakes, but you can't do anything about what happened yesterday. Living guilty or condemned will not make anything better. It's time to move forward and renew your mind with new thinking.

It's easy to go around with a "poor old me" mentality, feeling sorry for yourself, but when you drop the old negative baggage, not only will you feel a weight lifted off you but you will step into a new chapter of your life.

The scripture says, in 2 Corinthians, "Where the spirit of the Lord is, there is freedom." It doesn't say where the spirit of the Lord was. So, if you are always thinking about yesterday, last month, or last year, there is no freedom there; that is where the spirit of the Lord was.

You might have gone through some disappointments or made some mistakes, but decide today that you will not waste any more time worrying about what you could have done better, feeling angry over what didn't work out, upset over what went wrong. This is a new day; there are new opportunities ahead, so stop living in the past and start living in the present.

Living in regret, going over what you should have done, is not productive. Living upset, offended, or frustrated over what didn't work out will only limit your abilities.

Sometimes it is necessary to drop the offence, drop the blame, forget about the failure, and say, "I'm not carrying this negative baggage anymore. I'm going to live my life free. I'm leaving what was and coming over into what is." If somebody did you wrong, let God be their judge; if you made mistakes, quit beating yourself up and receive God's mercy. It's always available.

If you worked hard but didn't get the promotion or you did your best but the relationship didn't work out, instead of letting it affect you be mature enough to say, "Lord, I don't understand it, but I trust you. I know that it will work out to my advantage. So, I am not going to let anger annoyance of bitterness get the better of me. I'm not going to live my life always looking back. I'm going to keep moving forward, knowing that my best days are still ahead."

When you begin to renew your mind with new thinking, everything in your life will change.

A Lesson from Canaan

After Moses led the Israelites out of Egypt, God led them to the land He had promised. When the whole nation of Israel was camped at the edge of Canaan, the Lord said to Moses, "Send men out to explore the land I am giving them." So Moses sent out twelve spies, one leader from each of their ancestors' tribes, with specific instructions.

"See what the land is like and whether the people who live there are strong or weak, few or many. What kind of land do they live in? Is it good or bad? What kind of towns do they live in? Are they unwalled or fortified? How is the soil? Is it fertile or poor? Are there trees in it or not? Do your best to bring back some of the fruit of the land." Numbers 13:18–20

They returned from searching Canaan after forty days. Ten of the spies reported to Moses and the whole Israelite community, " We went into the land to which you sent us, and it does flow with milk and honey! Here is its fruit. But the people who live there are powerful, and the cities are fortified and very large... Numbers 13:27–28.

God had already said it was their land, but notice what they were thinking—weak, defeated, and fearful thoughts.

Joshua and Caleb, the other two spies, came back with a different attitude. They silenced the people before Moses and said, "We should go up and take possession of the land, for we can certainly do it. Yes, the people of the land are big, but we know that our God is bigger. Let us go at once and take it. We are well able."

But the ten men spoke up again, "We can't attack those people; they are stronger than we are." And they spread among the Israelites a bad report about the land they had explored. They said, "The land we explored devours those living in it. All the people we saw there are of great size. We seemed like grasshoppers in our own eyes, and we looked the same to them." Numbers 13:31–33

What I find interesting is Joshua and Caleb saw the same giants as the other ten spies. They saw the same problems, the same opposition, the same land, but instead of thinking defeated thoughts, they chose to think powerful thoughts. They weren't any bigger than the other spies; they didn't have more training, more experience, or weapons. The only difference was their thinking.

The negative news from the ten spies spread throughout the Israelites' camp and, before long, the whole Israelite community who had escaped slavery from Egypt were afraid and worried. They said to Moses, "Let's go back to Egypt, let's go back to being slaves."

That's how powerful having a negative attitude can be; ten men infected the minds of a nation. That is the same as the media today; a few networks can keep an entire country in fear.

As it turned out, because of their disbelief, the Israelites ended up wandering the desert for the next forty years; only Joshua and Caleb were allowed into the Promised Land. The lesson to take away from this story is to be careful how you think; don't become so infected by fear that you miss your destiny.

Stepping Forward

Are you like one of the ten spies looking at your current challenges through the lens of fear? "I can't see how things can get better. I'll never accomplish my dreams; I don't have the connections or the resources."

Or are you like Joshua and Caleb? You see the challenges that lie before you, but you have the faith to know that all will work out as God has planned. He has already promised that He will be with you. That He will protect you and give you strength. That He will provide for you, give you peace, and always love you. So don't get stuck in a fearful, defeated mindset.

Yes, current events look big, but our God is bigger. He parted the red seas, He brought the dead back to life, He saved three men from the fiery furnace. A pandemic is no match for him. A virus can be powerful, but our God is all-powerful.

I'm asking you to be like the two spies, Joshua, and Caleb, and think power thoughts, think can-do thoughts. Think thoughts of victory. In prayer, ask for wisdom, ask for guidance, ask for calmness and peace to guide you on your way.

When everyone around you is fearful, speak words of faith. You may be the only voice of faith they hear.

Have You Missed Your Destiny?

Like in the story of the Promised Land, you will find that most people, when difficulties come their way, will focus on the negative, telling you how big the problem is, how it won't get better, how you should settle where you are. But if you are going to fulfil your destiny, you must go against the grain. You can't just follow everyone and be afraid like most people, complain like your co-workers, be negative like your neighbour.

God is looking for people of faith, people like Joshua and Caleb; He is looking for people willing to stand out, people who believe when everyone else is fearful, who aren't discouraged by how big the problem is.

Negative people can easily affect you; you will have to guard your mind because negative news spreads faster than good news. Joshua and Caleb said, "We will be more than able," but that news didn't go very far.

But when the Israelites heard that the people of Canaan were huge, that they didn't have a chance, that news spread fast throughout the camp. Negative thinking is contagious.

All around us, there is negative news telling us how bad the virus is, how bad the economy is, what might happen and how it may get much worse with the new variants. I'm not faulting the news reporters; they're only doing their jobs. It's good to be up to date with global affairs, but you can't allow that poison to stay in your spirit. If you keep dwelling on the headlines, you will end up afraid, worried, panicked, thinking you're not going to make it.

When you focus on negative thoughts, they grow in your mind, which draws in more fear, more worry, and more defeat.

The Mo-bot

I enjoy running, as I find it beneficial for both body and mind. I often run a particular route; it takes almost an hour and sets me up for the day. Most of the road is flat, but there is one steep hill at the end. Getting up that hill requires all my focus and inner strength.

Even though it's difficult, I enjoy the challenge. But one day I was tired, I wasn't sleeping that well. About five minutes into my run, the hill started to play on my mind. I experienced thoughts like, "I don't want to go up that hill, I don't feel like it, I don't think I have the strength." I kept dreading it, telling myself over and over how hard it was going to be, wondering if I could make it up there. Then I received a phone call; I answered it on my Apple watch, slowing down my pace to have a conversation. About twenty minutes later, I hung up. My mind went straight back to thinking about the hill, only to notice that I had already run up it.

But because I was distracted, not focused on how hard it would be, I made it up the hill without a problem. My muscles weren't sore; I wasn't winded. I didn't feel any more tired than before. I didn't even remember going up it.

It got me thinking, how many things are we telling ourselves that we can't do? I can't handle this challenge; I can't change now at my age; I can't handle that difficult conversation. It is going to be uncomfortable.

We all dread certain things, thinking weak, defeated thoughts when the truth is we already have the strength to do all things. When God created you, He gave you everything you needed to fulfil your destiny; now quit telling yourself what you can't do, how it's never going to change. Negative thoughts drain your energy.

Instead, take time each day to praise God and be grateful for what you have. Then, when you face the hills of life, you will get over them easier than you thought.

Every morning, when you wake, you need to power up and get your mind going in the right direction. You must think faithful thoughts on purpose because if you believe whatever comes to your mind, thoughts will tell you that you have too many problems; that you're too tired and you'll never overcome that obstacle. So, before you check your phone or listen to the morning news, you need to think powerful thoughts, victory thoughts, can-do thoughts on purpose.

"I am strong, I am confident, I can handle anything that comes my way. I have the favour of God. This is going to be a good day."

Make it a point from today to focus your mind on victory first thing in the morning. The thoughts we think regularly can either lead us down the path of hope, joy, and victory or lead us down the path of fear, discouragement and hopelessness.

One of the ways that we can correct the course of our thoughts is by changing our words. David knew the powerful combination of thoughts and confession. He prayed, "Let the words of my mouth, and the meditation of my heart, be acceptable in thy sight, O Lord, my strength, and my redeemer" in Psalm 19:14. Today, I encourage you to declare and meditate on this faith-filled confession—

I declare that God loves me and has good plans for my life. Nothing I face will be too much for me. Through Christ I am full of power, strength, and determination. I will overcome every obstacle, outlast every challenge, and come through every difficulty. I will not worry; I will not doubt I will keep my trust in the Lord. Knowing that He will not fail me. And with His favour I will become everything He has created me to be.

Friend, you don't have to live your life weighed down by the heaviness of guilt, resentment, doubt, and worry any longer. You can live a life of joy, peace, and happiness.

Decide today: I'm not going to hold on to the bitterness, offence, or negative thinking anymore; I will make room for the good things that God wants to do in me and through me. I choose to renew my mind and release my faith.

Proverbs 3:5–6

So, trust in the Lord with all your heart and lean not on your own understanding, in all your ways submit to him and he will make your paths straight.

Thoughts Contain Power

Pay attention to what your mind is focusing on. Are you thinking power thoughts or are you thinking defeated thoughts? Awareness is the key.

If thoughts are negative, discouraging, fearful, don't give them the time of day. Turn them around and dwell on what God says about you. That He will always give you the grace, the strength and the faith for whatever comes your way.

Thoughts will whisper, *Nothing good is in your future; you have seen your best days, don't waste your time.* But if you dwell on those thoughts, you'll miss your destiny.

Turn the thoughts of defeat around and think thoughts of faith. *Something good is going to happen to me today. Favour is surrounding me like a shield. Goodness and mercy are flowing into my life.*

When you're going through tough times, the enemy will work overtime to convince you that the problem is too big. That you'll never get a job you enjoy; that your relationship will never get better; that your anxiety will never improve.

The enemy knows that if he can keep you defeated in your thoughts, he will keep you defeated in your life. The battle is taking place in your mind.

Thoughts will tell you, *It will never change, just give up on that dream, you can't take it anymore.* But instead of thinking those weak thoughts, drawing in more weakness, turn it around and think powerful thoughts.

"Yes, the problem looks big, but I have been armed with strength for every battle. I'm full of can-do power. What God started in my life, He will finish. This difficulty didn't come to stay. It came to pass."

But if you let fear, worry or doubt take control, you will feel overwhelmed, and if you dwell on the negativity, you will get stuck where you are. Pay attention to what is going on in your mind; you have more control than you realise.

Ephesians 4:22–24

You were taught, with regard to your former way of life, to put off your old self, which is being corrupted by its deceitful desires; to be made new in the attitude of your minds; and to put on the new self, created to be like God in true righteousness and holiness.

The Journey of Renewal

Romans 12:2 tells us that we shouldn't conform to the world's way of thinking. Instead, we should renew our minds. It wasn't until I learned how to do so did, I see change and manifest God's promises in my life.

I knew that to experience the life that God called me to live, I would have to remove my anxious thoughts and self-limiting beliefs. Here are the steps that I took to renew my mind and cast out negative thoughts.

1) Learn the thoughts that God thinks towards you

Most people want to stop their negative thinking, but, in my opinion, this is the wrong approach. To renew your mind and release your faith, you need to feed your mind with new thinking purposely.

Thoughts of faith, thoughts of gratitude, thoughts of trust.

John 15:1-4

"I am the true vine, and my Father is the gardener. He cuts off every branch in me that bears no fruit, while every branch that does bear fruit, he prunes so that it will be even more fruitful. You are already clean because of the word I have spoken to you. Remain in me, as I also remain in you. No branch can bear fruit by itself; it must remain in the vine. Neither can you bear fruit unless you remain in me.

It is so easy to dwell on negative thinking, and when you do, there will be endless people that will hold the same view as you. But to bear the fruit of faith, you must remain in the vine, you must keep your focus on faith, you must keep your focus on God.

Once you learn how to adopt the mindset of Christ, He will instil in you a confidence that can't be shaken, to move forward with His plan for your life.

2) Determine what kind of mindset you currently have

There are two kinds of mindset: a fixed mindset and a growth mindset. The fixed mindset is the most common and the most harmful, so it's worth understanding how it can affect you. In a fixed mindset, you believe your character, intelligence, and abilities are static, meaning you can't change. You may say things like, "She naturally has strong faith and confidence," or "I'm just no good at developing myself."

In a growth mindset, you believe "Anyone that does enough work can be good at anything. That by renewing your mind in Christ, you will be a new creation.

When you have a growth mindset, you thrive on challenges and see failure not as negative but part of the journey. Helping you to grow and stretch your existing abilities.

When I had to organise the extension for my dad, I was thinking anxious and self-sabotaging thoughts; I was engaged in a fixed, stagnant mindset. I wanted to move forward, but my thoughts prevented me from taking the steps. Fear has the power to stop you in your tracks. I had to learn how to renew my thought processes towards my situation by adopting a growth mindset.

3) Cast out the negative thoughts

A lot of us are stuck in a fixed mindset because we are letting the enemy win. We aren't fighting back when he is attacking our minds. It's time that you pick up you're only weapon, God's Word, and fight back.

2 Corinthians 10:5 tells us to capture our thoughts and teach them how to obey Christ. How can we do that? By adhering to *Philippians 4:8-9*

"And now, dear brothers and sisters, one final thing. Fix your thoughts on what is true, and honourable, and right, and pure, and lovely, and admirable. Think about things that are excellent and worthy of praise. Keep putting into practice all you learned and received from me— everything you heard from me and saw me doing. Then the God of peace will be with you."

Paul broke it down for us. Think about what is true, excellent, and praiseworthy. Put it into practice. Then the peace of God will help you sustain those thoughts. Sometimes that can be easier said than done, so here is an exercise for you.

Exercise in Renewal

First identify the thought you would like to cast out. Let say, anxiety. Look up what God's Word says about anxiety. For example, Philippians 4:6-7 ESV.

Do not be anxious about anything, but in everything by prayer and supplication with thanksgiving let your requests be made known to God. And the peace of God, which surpasses all understanding, will guard your hearts and your minds in Christ Jesus.

Then write down what it is saying to you?

Pray with thanksgiving and let your requests be made known to God. So, your prayer is not simply, please give me what I need, but thank you for everything you have done for me in the past. I am very grateful, could you please help me again.

Prayer for Anxiety

Dear Lord, thank you for the times in my life that I was without these anxious feelings, please help me to experience them times again.

When you pray in this way, as Apostle Paul sets out, the peace of God, which surpasses all understanding, will guard your hearts and your minds.

4) Determine the thoughts you need to think to manifest your desired outcome

It's not enough to cast out negative thoughts. As I have mentioned before, you must intentionally feed your mind with new thoughts, so your focus is not on want you don't want, but on what you do want, peace of mind, health, and happiness. Replacing the fear with not only God's Word but with positive thoughts.

If you want to feel peace of mind, write down the thoughts that support that feeling. Examples, "I attract loving and positive people into my life. All situations in my life will work out for the greater good."

5) Write a list of affirmations/scriptures

Write down the prayers, thoughts, and scriptures from this chapter to keep on hand whenever you need them. Keep them on your desk at work. Get a whiteboard marker and write them as reminders on your mirror. Bottom line, you must get super focused. You need to have ammunition to fight the enemy's attacks.

6) Know your weaknesses

If you know a particular area you are struggling in, prepare a custom list of thoughts, affirmations, and scriptures to focus on when you find yourself struggling with your weaknesses.

7) Grace, grace, grace

Last but not least, remember to show yourself grace. You will have bad days, but you must be prepared to do what it takes to snap yourself out of it on those days. Ring a friend, go for an adventure, through a forest or to the beach. Don't allow yourself to stay in that dark place.

Each day is a new chance to renew your mind and spirit.

Releasing Your Faith

The first step to designing a life you desire is to renew your mind as your thoughts influence everything you do. Sometimes people will say to me, "I've tried hard, I've prayed; I've done this, I've done that, but I haven't had much success. What more can I do?

Well, let's begin with mind management. What changes can you make in the structure of your thinking? Can you get into your mind and see how it works, determining what thoughts need to be downloaded, installed and what ideas need to be removed?

If you are worried all day, every day, then those thoughts have to go. And the way to do that is to ask yourself these questions: Can I change the situation I am worried about? If yes, get to work on that without delay. If no, why are you worrying? If you can't change the outcome, worrying is a waste of time and energy.

It says in scripture, as a man thinketh in his heart, so is he. Meaning, each of us, by working upon renewing our minds can remake our life, and transform our circumstances.

You can change your hair, clothing, or spouse, but if you don't change your mind, the same set of experiences will keep repeating over and over because everything outwardly may have changed, but nothing inwardly changed.

If you feel depressed at this time, you must back up and work out what you are thinking about because thoughts of worry and doubt will determine how you feel. And how you feel determines how your life will work out.

If you feel low, you need to ask yourself, "what am I thinking about, and how long have I been thinking about it?" How long you think about something is called focus, and whatever you focus on, you give strength to. If you focus on your weaknesses or past failures, you strengthen those things, meaning they have greater power over your life.

Isaiah 41:10
Do not fear for I am with you do not be dismayed for I am your God. I will strengthen you and help you, I will uphold you with my righteous right hand.

Today, some of you are worried about the threat of trouble, the threat of what might happen, what could happen, and it's wearing you down. I will let you in on a little secret; most of what you are worrying about will never happen. But, if you allow those thoughts to dwell in your mind, those thoughts will rob your peace, stealing your joy and your happiness.

Negative thinking can rob you of your life— because you can *think* your way into a nervous breakdown, *think* your way into depression. *Think* your way into defeat.

Many of us have strongholds in our minds. A stronghold is a way of thinking and feeling that has developed a life of its own. You don't want to worry, but it's a habit. You don't want to live in fear or be doubtful, but you can't help it.

For this to change, you need to form new habits, and you do this by renewing your mind, so that your faith can be released. Forgive yourself for past mistakes. Forgive others that have hurt you. Unforgiveness is a stronghold that will consume you if you allow it.

I want to challenge you to waste no more time, no more effort, no more strength focusing on the past, locked in old thinking; your destiny is far too important. You don't have to live weighted down by the heaviness of anger, regret or fear any longer.

Decide today that you are not going to hold onto the negative thinking anymore, that you are going to make room for the good things that God wants to do with you and through you.

I'm asking you to be a Joshua, be a Caleb, and move forward in faith knowing that all will work out as God has planned. Speak faith over your life and the people around you. And in prayer, ask with gratitude, for guidance, wisdom, and peace of mind. If you do this, I believe and declare that the chains holding you back will be removed, and your life will be filled with health, happiness, and joy.

Move forward with positive expectancy and watch amazing things flow into your life.

Jeremiah 29:11
For I know the plans I have for you declares the Lord, plans to prosper you and not to harm you, plan to give you hope and a future.

ABOUT THE AUTHOR

I live on the northwest coast of Ireland. I use this medium to share my true voice. I wish to enlighten others and help them to see that God wants the very best for them. We often make it hard for him to enter our lives as we focus on the dark clouds rather than the silver lining.

In this growing digital frontier I just want to shed a little light out into the world to light up peoples lives in the hope that they to will help inspire others which will slowly but surely change the world, even in a small way.

My Other Books

God's Perfect Timing
The Power Of Letting Go
The Power Of Choice
The Power Of Words
Make Space for God